Finding Out About
THE COAST

John Bentley and
Bill Charlton

Batsford Academic and Educational *London*

~~~Contents~~~

© John Bentley and Bill Charlton 1985
First published 1985

Typeset by Tek-Art Ltd, Kent
and printed in Great Britain
by R.J. Acford
Chichester, Sussex
for the publishers
Batsford Academic and Educational,
an imprint of B. T. Batsford Ltd,
4 Fitzhardinge Street
London W1H 0AH

ISBN 0 7134 4426 6

ACKNOWLEDGMENTS

The Authors and Publishers thank the following for their kind permission to reproduce the illustrations: Imray Laurie Norie and Wilson Ltd, page 37 (from Imray Yachting Chart C29 based upon BA Chart No. 1612 with the sanction of the Controller, HM Stationery Office and of the Hydrographer of the Navy); Newnes Books, page 35 (from *Lifeboat by* P. Howarth, 1981); the Ordnance Survey, pages 19, 21. All other photographs and diagrams in the book and on the cover are copyright of the Authors. Special thanks are expressed to John Marshall for the photographic prints.

Cover picture
The colour picture on the front cover is of Bude, Cornwall.

For all those people who live on islands, the coast and the sea have a special meaning. They help to give people a sense of being a separate community. They may also give a feeling of protection. In those unhappy years when the countries of Europe were at war, people in Britain saw the coastline as a symbol of their independence and freedom. Nowadays, British people are sometimes criticized by others (by our partners in the EEC, for example) for being "insular" – that is, for thinking too much about our own interests and not enough about our responsibilities in the wider world. Perhaps they are right. Perhaps we still do think of the sea as a barrier which helps us to keep ourselves to ourselves. What do you think?

When people talk of the "coast", they mean, in a general sort of way, the place where the land meets the sea. The word "seaside" is used like this too. What is it that makes the coast such a special kind of place? It isn't just the edge of the water and the waves that come to mind, even if that is the most important bit. There's also the sea beyond the water's edge, with sailing boats and wind-surfers, perhaps, and bigger ships in the distance. On the land side there may be a beach or promenade, a caravan park or camp-site – or even a town, with shops and amusement arcades. And what about the traffic jams on a Bank Holiday? They may be a kilometre or more from the edge of the sea but they are probably the first indication that you have arrived at the "coast". The coast, then, is not a narrow, restricted place, where you can stand with one foot in the sea and one on the land – it's a zone, starting a little way out to sea, and finishing a little way inland.

The coast is a very important "resource", that is, something which can be used to our advantage, or benefit. An obvious example is the way in which the coast has been used (or "developed", as we say) to provide us with leisure and holiday activities. In this case, the things which are important are cliffs, bays, beaches, waves and so on. The coast has other kinds of resources, too. It has ports, for example, which provide us with opportunities to trade with other countries. Also, for some kinds of industry (e.g. steel works and power stations) low-lying land near the coast is the most suitable kind of place for siting their factories and equipment. In this book you will be finding out about some of these coastal resources.

It sometimes happens that one way of using a stretch of the coast will spoil the coast for other purposes – building a power-station, for instance, on an area of salt-marsh that is important for bird-life. One of our biggest problems is how to make the best decision when this kind of conflict arises. Organizing the most satisfactory use of the coast is called "coastal management". Towards the end of the book you will be asked to think about this problem.

Whatever it is that we may want to do with any particular part of the coast much depends on what the natural conditions are like, and how they are likely to change. For that reason the first part of the book concentrates on finding out about natural features and processes at the coast. We need to know how the coast has been formed, in case this has any bearing on how we want to use it.

You will not need any special equipment to follow the suggestions made in the book. A notebook, pencil, measuring tape, plastic bags and magnifying glass will be sufficient. You will, however, be asked to consult maps and search for information in libraries. Sometimes you have to contact government or council offices. Most of the information you will

~Useful Sources~

collect, though, will be what you can see while you are out and about along the coast. This kind of study is called "field-work".

Much of the finding out can be done on your own, but field-work is always more interesting – and more fun – if you work with someone else or in a small group. If you have different views and ideas you can discuss and argue. However, whether you are on your own, or in a group, you must remember that the coast can be a dangerous place. Always check your plans with your parents or other responsible grown-ups who know the area before you set out on your field-work.

PLACES TO VISIT

Wherever you live there will be a variety of places to visit which are concerned with the coast. To find out which are close to your area ask your local librarian for guidance. Here are some typical examples of places worth visiting as part of your project.

The *Cutty Sark* and National Maritime Museum, Greenwich, London
The Thames Barrier, Woolwich, London
HMS *Victory* at Portsmouth, Hampshire
Shipyards (e.g. Wallsend, Newcastle-on-Tyne)
Grace Darling Museum (R.N.L.I.), Bamburgh, Northumberland
Dungeness Lighthouse, Kent
Cromer Lifeboat Museum, Norfolk
Custom's House Museum, Great Yarmouth, Norfolk
The Maritime Museum, Lowestoft
H.M. Dockyard, Plymouth, Devon

Local seaside churches and churchyards often have memorials to seamen and lifeboat men.

The main purpose of the activities described in this book is to encourage you to explore the coast and make your own discoveries. A lot of information is already there in the landscape around you, but, to help you pursue your investigations, the following further sources of information are given as guidance.

1. SEASIDE VISITS
At the coast there will be local officials and organizations that can help you. Here are a few of them: the Harbour Master's Office; the Pier authorities; the local coastguard and lifeboat stations; the tourist office or local publicity officer of the town. If there are docks or a port of entry for overseas travellers there will also be officers of H.M. Customs and Excise and dockyard authorities. Remember, too, to visit the local fishmarket and to talk with some of the fishermen.

2. MAPS AND CHARTS
Maps of the coast, the shore and the coastal waters can be rich sources of information. The more you use them the more valuable you will find them.

(i) *Ordnance Survey Maps* The Ordnance Survey has a range of maps available at different scales. The large-scale plans and maps are best for the study of the seaside town itself. On the 1 : 2,500 (40 cm to 1 km) and the 1 : 10,000 (10 cm to 1 km) you can identify the major buildings and streets of the town. The physical shape and features of the coastal zone are more usefully studied on the smaller map scales.

On the 1 : 25,000 (4 cm to 1 km), for example, the separate zones of the shore, the dunes, cliffs, wave-cut platforms, etc, can be easily identified. On the 1 : 50,000 (2 cm to 1 km) the larger area covered by this smaller scale allows you to see the shape of the whole coastline, the pattern of headlands and bays and the distribution of coastal settlements.

Information about the Ordnance Survey maps is available from the Director General, The Ordnance Survey, Romsey Road, Maybush, Southampton SO9 4DH.

(ii) *Admiralty Charts* Maps of the coastal and offshore waters are known as navigation charts. They show the specialized information needed by mariners, such as water depth, tidal range, location of reefs and navigational aids (buoys, lighthouses, etc). Admiralty charts can be purchased from shops specializing in marine supplies, or consulted at local libraries. One publisher of popular marine charts is Imray Laurie Norie and Wilson Ltd, Wych House, St Ives, Huntingdon, Cambridgeshire.

(iii) *Geology Maps and Booklets* The coastline with cliffs and rocky foreshore is the best place to start to pursue an interest in geology. Information about geology maps and publications is available from the Geological Museum, Exhibition Road, South Kensington, London SW7. Some of their books are given in the list at the end of this book.

(iv) *Atlases* A good atlas will give you many useful facts about coasts. The significant points of some topics (e.g. ferry routes or the fetch of waves) can only be grasped if you study an atlas.

3. NATIONAL ORGANIZATIONS
The following government and national bodies can provide useful information for your projects:

(i) *Trade and Economy (ports, overseas trade, etc)*
Information Division,
Department of Trade and Industry,
1 Victoria Street, London SW1H 0ET

Fisheries Department,
Great Westminster House,
Horseferry Road, London SW1P 2AE

H.M. Board of Customs and Excise,
King's Beam House,
39-41 Mark Lane, London EC3R 7HE

(ii) *Safety, Navigation and Rescue*
Trinity House, Tower Hill, London EC3

H.M. Coastguard, 8th Floor, Sunley House, High Holborn, London WC1

Royal National Lifeboat Institution,
West Quay Road, Poole, Dorset BH15 1HZ

(iii) *Planning, Protection and Conservation of Coasts*
Department of Environment (planning policies for coasts),
2 Marsham Street, London SW1P 3EB
(There are also regional offices in Birmingham, Bristol, Leeds, Manchester, Newcastle, Northern Ireland and Nottingham.)

National Trust (Enterprise Neptune),
42 Queen Anne's Gate, London SW1H 9AS

Countryside Commission (Heritage Coasts),
John Dower House, Crescent Place, Cheltenham, Glos GL50 3RA

Royal Society for the Protection of Birds,
The Lodge, Sandy, Beds SG19 2DL

(iv) *Maritime History*
National Maritime Museum,
Greenwich, London SE10 9NF

4. LOCAL SOURCES OF INFORMATION
Two very useful sources of information are the local authorities and the local libraries and museums.

(i) Local authorities which have coastal areas within their boundaries have responsibilities for the management and protection of the coast. The most useful department to approach initially is the planning department where large-scale plans and planning proposals can be consulted. Departments responsible for recreation and engineering work can also help you. If there are harbour and port facilities in the area these will have information officers. Responsibilities for coastal management are also held by local water authorities.

(ii) The names and addresses of authorities similar to these can be obtained from your local library. As a general rule, the best place to start any local study is the library enquiry desk. Amongst the many reference books on coasts, the following books are generally available, or can be obtained for you.

Brown's Registrations (fishing boat registration numbers)
Imray Yachting Charts
Lloyd's Register of Shipping
Lloyd's Register of Yachts
Macmillan's Nautical Almanac
Reed's Nautical Almanac
Stanford's Charts

The Librarian will also have information about local museums and interest groups concerned with the coastal environment.

5. Finally, there are newspapers, journals and magazines which contain news items and articles concerned directly or indirectly with coastal activities (e.g. sea-rescue or wind-surfing). You could keep a scrapbook of newspaper cuttings. An enquiry at your local newsagent's will give you some idea of the range of magazines available.

Models of the Coast

You are going to begin your study of coasts by looking at those parts which are closest to the water's edge. As you might expect, the land which lies immediately next to the sea is where the influence of the sea is greatest. When you come to study it in detail you will find that you can divide this part of the coast into a number of quite distinct sections or zones. These zones are illustrated in the diagrams on these pages, but if you compare the details with places you know well, you may find that one or more of the zones shown in the diagrams are missing. These diagrams (which are called cross sections) are meant to represent "models" of the coast, so they have to include all the zones you might possibly find. Comparing a "real" coast with the "model" coast is a useful way to learn about the special words which are used to describe the different zones.

Notice that in the diagrams the "shore" is divided into three sections. The central part is called the "foreshore". This is a zone which alternates between land and sea because when the tide is in, it is covered by water and when the tide is out, it becomes land. On the seaward side of the foreshore is a zone which is constantly covered with water. This is the "offshore". Then there is a zone above the high-tide mark which is only occasionally reached by the sea during storms, and is called the "backshore".

We divide coasts into two general kinds, depending upon whether the relief of the land is high or low. That is why we have two diagrams. On the one hand, where the relief is high, the scenery often contains cliffs and rocks. On the other hand, low coasts often have zones of sand dunes and salt-marsh. Notice that both kinds of coast have a "beach" and an "inter-tidal zone". In some parts of Britain (e.g. north Yorkshire) a high coast will extend for tens of kilometres before it changes to a low coast. In other places the two types alternate over a distance of just a few kilometres (e.g. in parts of Sussex).

When you study a stretch of coast, try to decide which of these two "models" most closely fits your real example. Find a place where you can get to the water's edge, turn round and walk directly inland, bearing the diagrams in mind and noting any distinct zones. Then move a few hundred metres along the coast and do the exercise again. Is the pattern the same or different? Are there any man-made features which interrupt the succession of natural zones?

If you are unable to make a real visit, you can study a coast in your imagination, provided you have an Ordnance Survey map on a scale of 1:50,000 or 1:25,000 with a coastline on it. Look at the key, find all the symbols which are used to show coastal features and make a careful copy of them. Choose a section of coast (say, 5 km) and make a list of all the coastal features you can find there. Use your list to write a description of a walk along the coast you have chosen.

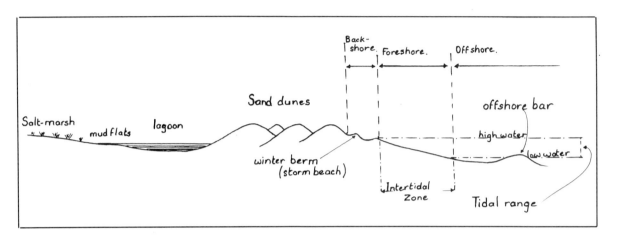

A coast of low relief with features of deposition.

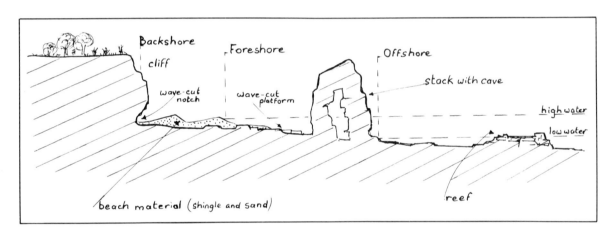

A coast of high relief with features of erosion.

Waves

As you may know, all moving objects possess energy. Waves possess energy because they are made of moving water. When you go bathing in a rough sea, the energy in a big wave may be enough to knock you over. This wave energy is important because it helps to shape some of the features we find at the coast. Waves pick up their energy from the wind as it blows against the surface of the sea. To build up really good waves the wind has to blow from the same direction for several days, ideally from a direction where there is a long stretch of uninterrupted water. At any point on the coast, the distance which a wind has travelled across water before it reaches land is called the "fetch". The longer the fetch, the better the chance of big waves with lots of energy.

You can see here the curling crest of the wave, the surf of the breaker and, in the foreground, the thin spread of the swash as it swirls up the slope of the beach. Estimate the distance over which the wave's energy is used up (i.e. from the breaker to the edge of the swash).

When a wave breaks against the shore, its energy is used up in pushing the water up the beach. The water which foams up the beach is called the "swash". Some of it sinks into the beach and the rest – the "backwash" – flows back into the sea. Swash and backwash are important because they move material up and down the beach. You can feel this happening when you paddle, even in little waves near the water's edge. When the swash surges over your feet you feel the bits of sand washing against you, and if you stand in the backwash the undertow is sometimes strong enough to suck the sand from beneath you. The undertow is sometimes so strong that it is too dangerous to go bathing.

Where the swash is more powerful than the backwash, the amount of sand which is pushed up onto the beach is greater than that which is removed. These waves, which *add* material to the beach, are called "constructive" waves. Those with a stronger backwash *remove* material from the beach and are "destructive" waves.

If waves approach the shore obliquely (sideways on), they move material *along* the shore. You can find out how this process works by doing an experiment with a small ball (e.g. a tennis ball). Put the ball on the water's edge just in front of the breaking wave. The swash will carry the ball *up and along* the beach, and the backwash will take it back down again. Each new swash will repeat the process and you may find that you have moved quite a way along the beach. This process of moving sand and shingle along the coast is called "long-shore drifting". At seaside resorts where people want to have a good-sized beach to enjoy, groynes are built out into the sea to stop long-shore drifting from sweeping the beaches away.

The next time you are going to visit the coast,

Groynes are built to trap shingle and slow down the movement of beach materials along the shore. From the difference in the width of the beach can you tell the direction of the long-shore drift?

use your atlas beforehand to find out the direction of the longest fetch of that particular part of the coast. When you get there, try to work out from which direction the waves are approaching, and whether this is the same as the wind direction. If there are any groynes built out into the sea, compare the amount of sand and shingle on each side and work out the direction of long-shore drifting at that part of the coast.

Tides

Anyone who has visited the seaside in Britain will know what a dramatic effect tides can have on the appearance of the coast. In some places the sea goes out so far that you can hardly see it and people at the water's edge look more like ants. A harbour full of water, with boats bobbing up and down, looks a completely different place at low tide when the boats are stranded on the mud.

In most places the tides ebb (go out) and flow (come in) twice a day. This rise and fall is caused by the gravitational pull of the Sun and Moon on the waters of the ocean – that is why the pattern of the tides is linked with the phases of the Moon. (You can find a full scientific explanation of tides in an encyclopaedia.) When there is a great difference between the level of the water at high and at low tide, the tides are known as "spring" tides. When there is least difference, the tides are called "neap" tides.

Tides are important because of the effects of the regular rise and fall of the sea-level on the way people work and play at the coast. Anyone who works with ships, for example, needs to know the times of the tides very accurately

because of the effect which they have on the depth of the water in harbours and shipping lanes. For this reason, "tide tables" are published, giving the times of high and low tide for all places around the coast on every day of the year. The tide tables used on ships are very detailed, but simplified tables are published in many newspapers (e.g. *The Times*).

Study the tide tables and find out how the pattern of high and low tides varies around the coasts of Britain. Compare the times of high tide at the places mentioned in the tables and

This is the office of the Pier Master at Broadstairs, Kent. What is the difference in time between "high water a.m." and "high water p.m."?

find out which way the tides move around our coasts. Then compare the times of consecutive high tides at one place and work out how many hours and minutes there are between one high tide and the next. When you next go on holiday at the seaside, you can consult the tide tables at the beginning of the week, and make a note of the changes in the tide from day to day. That way you will know the best times to go to the beach.

The difference between the levels of the sea at low tide and at high tide is called the "tidal range". Find out what the tidal range is at your part of the coast. If you can visit a harbour, you may be able to estimate the tidal range from marks on the harbour wall.

Many seaside activities are closely linked to the stages in the tides. See how many activities you can find at your part of the coast which are governed by the tide in this way.

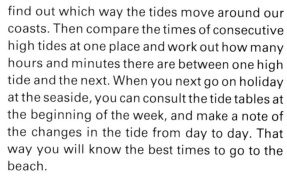

The tide is well out on this tidal section of the River Ely at Penarth. Estimate the difference in metres between the levels of high water and low water at this point.

11

Beaches

Generally speaking, people think of beaches as places – Blackpool beach, say, or Brighton beach. A beach is a place where you go for a swim, eat your ice-creams and generally have a good time. However, "beach" also has a technical meaning. It is the name given to all the various kinds of *material* which accumulate along the coast between the low-tide mark and the line of the highest tides. Beach materials, then, are found on the foreshore and the backshore.

Beach material consists of a mixture of sand and shingle (pebbles). The action of the sea in shaking the pebbles together is similar to what happens in a stone-polisher. That is why the pebbles are smooth and rounded. In addition to sand and shingle, beaches also contain all the pieces of timber and other rubbish washed up by the sea, and the shells of sea creatures.

Beaches are often worked into distinctive shapes by the action of the water and the wind. On sand beaches you will often find a pattern of narrow ridges in the damp sand below high water. These "ripple marks" are formed by the action of water as the tide goes out. Above high water, sand beaches sometimes have a zone of sand dunes formed from sand blown by the wind. On shingle beaches the limit of a high tide is often marked by a distinctive ridge in the pebbles, called a "berm". You will sometimes find a series of berms, each one marking the position of a previous high tide. Up on the backshore there may be a "storm beach" – a large ridge often containing boulders or tree trunks hurled up onto the backshore by the enormous power of storm waves. On beaches containing a mixture of sand and shingle,

Only the litter bins remain on the beach at the end of the day. What indications are there that the tide is out? Can you identify different zones of the shore in this photograph? Make a sketch of the picture and label it with the terms "foreshore", "offshore" and "backshore".

"cusps" may be formed, as in the right-hand photograph. Cusps are small embayments, a few metres across, with sand in the centre and ridged round with pebbles.

When you carry out a survey of beach materials, you should first find out the time of low tide so that you study the full width of the beach. Walk up from the water's edge as you did for the work on pages 6-7, but this time look out for any distinctive sand or shingle shapes in the beach. Note the position of these features by measuring or by pacing, and use your information to construct a cross section of the beach, drawn to scale (see pages 6-7). If your beach is a busy holiday beach, see if people use the various beach features in different ways.

On all beaches the size and composition of the beach material vary from one place to

As you walk along this shoreline near Bude, Cornwall, you can see the variation in size of beach materials, with sand, shingle and large boulders. The regular crescent embayments of the cusps are separated by thin ridges of shingle. What do you notice about the shape of the pebbles?

TABLE A

Size ranges of sediments (approximate diameter measurements)

Boulder	
—————— **256 mm** ——————	
Cobble	
—————— **64 mm** ——————	
Pebble	
—————— **60 mm** ——————	
Gravel	
—————— **2.0 mm** ——————	
Sand	
—————— **0.06 mm** ——————	
Silt	
—————— **0.002 mm** ——————	
Clay	

another. Find out what kind of variation there is on your beach by collecting samples of material systematically from, say, ten different locations. Put each sample in a plastic bag with a note of its location. Measure and compare the amounts of sand and pebbles, using the table on the left. When you have completed your work, write a paragraph to describe the results under the heading "Variations in Beach Material at ___".

On the south coast of England, there are two very famous beaches, one at Dungeness and the other at Chesil Beach. Find out from an encyclopaedia what is special about these beaches and write a paragraph about each of them, explaining how they were formed.

Cliffs and Caves

Cliffs and caves are spectacular and exciting features of coastal scenery and both are evidence of the destructive power of waves against the coast. Cliffs and caves are caused by erosion whereas beaches are the result of deposition.

Wave attack is concentrated into a fairly narrow section at the foot of cliffs – from just below the level of low tide to as high above the high-tide mark as storm waves reach. The waves erode a notch at the base of the cliffs and this undercutting eventually causes the upper part of the cliff to collapse. Then the process begins again and the line of the cliffs gradually recedes (retreats inland). The rate at which this happens depends on the resistance

of the rocks. In the Holderness area of Humberside, where the cliffs are made of clay, the coast has retreated 4 km since Roman times and several villages which existed in medieval times have been washed into the sea.

Most erosion takes place during storms. With strong on-shore winds and a long fetch, the energy released from a breaking wave may be equivalent to thousands of tonnes. The sheer explosive force of this energy will gradually weaken and destroy the rocks at the foot of a cliff. The work of erosion is helped by the sand and pebbles which are carried in the waves and which are also hurled at the cliff during storm conditions.

The rocks forming a cliff are never

This is a small headland near Watchet, Somerset. The different layers or strata of rock (sandstone, limestone and shale) are very evident. Each rock type has a different resistance to erosion and the cliff face shows very clearly what is known as differential erosion. Can you see the wave-cut notch at the base of the cliff?

completely uniform, so some parts erode more easily than others. Many rocks have natural lines of weakness called "joints" and "bedding planes", or they may have been broken by faults. These weaknesses are soon exposed by the forces of erosion. It is often the more rapid erosion of joints, bedding planes or faults that causes the development of caves.

If some sections of a cliff are particularly hard and resistant they may be left standing after the rocks around them have been eroded. You can sometimes see isolated blocks called "stacks" standing out in front of the main line of cliffs and forming little islands when the tide is in.

In many places along the coast you can find cliffs that are no longer being eroded by the sea because they stand so far back from the water that the waves never reach them. In seaside resorts, old cliffs like these are often developed as part of the amenities, with walks and viewpoints.

These large caves in the limestone cliffs of South Wales near Cardiff have been formed by waves eroding and enlarging a vertical crack known as a "joint". The horizontal lines in the cliff face are called bedding planes. Why is one of the people wearing a hard-hat?

If there are cliffs at your part of the coast, make an estimate of how high they are and find out what rocks they are made of (see pages 22-23). If the water reaches to the foot of the cliffs, see if you can find any signs of undercutting. Is there any collapsed material lying at the foot of the cliffs? Are there any caves? How far in do they go? Are there any stacks? Is there any sign of how far up the cliffs the waves reach? Above this level you may find that plants have been able to gain a foothold in pockets of soil. Find a good viewpoint and draw a sketch of the cliffs, labelling all the features you have recognized. Find out if the cliffs are used in any special way. If they are dangerous, how does the local council prevent accidents happening?

Rocks and Rock-pools

When erosion causes the line of a cliff to retreat (as we saw on pages 14-15), the rocks underlying the foot of the cliff still remain to show where the cliffs used to be. These rocks are often uncovered at low tide, when they form a kind of low platform in front of the present-day cliffs. Because of the way it has been formed, this is called a "wave-cut platform". Rocks are often one of the most fascinating parts of the coast, especially when they alternate with rock-pools of different shapes and sizes, each with its own mysterious collection of seaweed and sea creatures, and the whole area smelling strongly of the sea.

Erosion by the waves is very active on these rocky platforms. For that reason there is not usually much beach material to be found, except what has been trapped in crevices between the rocks. Wave-cut platforms are mostly to be seen in front of headlands or in other exposed parts of the coast.

Anybody who has ever enjoyed scrambling among seaside rocks knows that they vary considerably from one place to another. In some cases the rocks are smooth, and you can jump from one to another without worrying about falling. In other places the surface of the rocks is so sharp and irregular that you are likely to cut yourself if you slip. Sometimes shellfish attach themselves to the rocks. Sometimes the rock platform is almost level, with occasional humps; sometimes it is criss-crossed with deep, narrow chasms that make it difficult to find a way across. Where the platform extends out into the sea it often dips down below the water. A line of rocks hidden below the surface of the sea is called a "reef" and it can be a serious hazard for ships close into the shore.

Exploring the variety of life in the rock-pools is a favourite activity at the seaside. Each pool is like a small marine aquarium and provides an opportunity to study the plants and sea creatures that live at the edge of the sea. Find a suitable rock-pool and see how much life you can find in it. Make sketches in your note-book, together with brief descriptions, and then use a natural history reference book in your library to help you to identify what you found. Common rock-pool plants are sea lettuce, coraline seaweed, thong weed and kelp. Among these plants look for limpets, barnacles, shore-crabs

and the delicate form of the beadlet anemone.

The illustration on this page shows part of the coast of Cornwall. The photograph was taken at low tide and the rocky wave-cut platform is very conspicuous. This coastal scene also contains some of the features that have been mentioned in previous sections. Take a piece of plain paper (say 30cm x 20cm, or larger) and draw a sketch of the scene in the photograph, including in it the following features: cliff, beach, cusps, wave-cut platform, breakers, off-shore zone. Label all these features neatly and add what you think is a suitable title for your sketch.

This extensive wave-cut platform is at the southern end of Widemouth Bay on the north coast of Cornwall. What evidence is there of structure in the exposed rocks of the foreshore? (See pages 22-23.)

Salt-Marshes

Not all parts of the coast are being eroded by the sea and in some places the coast is actually being extended by the deposition of pebbles, sand or mud. This can only happen where the coast is protected from the force of waves and storms — in river estuaries, for example, or in sheltered bays.

Under these sheltered conditions, the finest silt and mud carried into the shore and deposited by the tides gradually build up into banks which are left above the water level at low tide. In time, salt-loving plants become established on these banks and they help to trap more silt so that more and more plants can grow. Gradually, over the years, areas of continuous vegetation are formed and the tidal waters are restricted into well-defined muddy channels. This kind of area is called a "salt-marsh".

Salt-marshes are not places where you can enjoy the fun of the seaside. People usually avoid them because they are so muddy. However, these salt-marshes form an especially valuable part of the coastal "wetlands" and for many creatures of the natural world they are a very important environment. For millions of birds, many of them migrants, salt-marshes provide habitats rich in food.

When a salt-marsh develops, a new coastline is formed. It is often quite easy to see where the old coastline used to be because there is usually quite a distinct rise from the low salt-marsh to slightly higher and drier land. Sometimes the alteration of a coastline in this way changes the economic life of the coast. Sandwich, in Kent, was a busy port during the Middle Ages, and it was one of the famous Cinque Ports. However, over the years the River Stour silted up and large areas of salt-

This salt-marsh is part of Pegwell Bay on the east coast of Kent. The dominant vegetation of spartina grass is typical of salt-marshes. What evidence is there to suggest that this salt-marsh is at an early stage of development?

marsh were formed where it enters Sandwich Bay. The mouth of the Stour became less suitable for shipping and the port gradually declined. Nowadays it is hardly used at all except by pleasure craft.

Areas of salt-marsh are marked on Ordnance Survey maps, so find out if any are marked on the map of your area of coast. Study the shape of the coastline and see if you can work out how the areas of salt-marsh have been protected from erosion by the sea. Go to visit the area (you may have to look carefully to find a suitable path) and make a study of its wildlife. See how many different plants and birds you can identify. The most typical plants besides the spartina grass are sea purslane, thrift and sea lavender. The common birds of the salt-marsh include the grey plover, the dunlin and the distinctively marked avocet. Search for the line of the junction between the salt-marsh and the former coastline and see if there is any evidence of previous activities which have now ceased. Visit your local library and find out if there are any old maps which show the earlier extent of the marshes. Compare the old map with a modern map and make careful copies from them to show any changes in the position and size of the marsh, noting the different dates. Is there any evidence to show that the use of the marshes has changed?

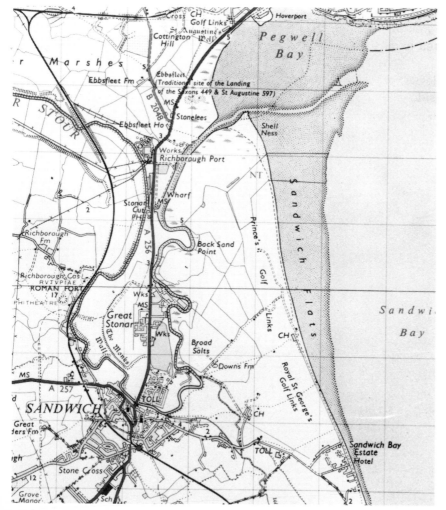

This map extract is from the O.S. Sheet 179 (1:50,000). How far from the present coastline is the old port of Sandwich, measured along the course of the River Stour? The photograph of the salt-marsh was taken from near the Hoverport located at the top of this map extract.

19

Sand Dunes

Sand dunes are often found along low-lying coasts where they may form a distinct zone sometimes called "warrens" or "burrows". They are heaped up from sand which has blown inland from the shore. In some places they consist of no more than low mounds, scarcely one metre high, making a patch no larger than a garden lawn. In other places they rise ten or twenty metres, reaching a hundred metres or more inland and extending for many kilometres along the coast.

Coastal dunes form best where there is a wide foreshore, which dries out between high tides, and regular on-shore winds. You often find a line of sand dunes at the head of a bay, especially if the slope of the shore is gentle. (Why do you think the slope makes a difference?) Sand is blown inland from the beach and gets trapped in the vegetation beyond the backshore. As the dunes grow in size, some kinds of vegetation (especially marram grass) manage to keep on growing

through the sand and this helps to bind the sand together.

The map shows the area around Oxwich Bay in South Wales. Oxwich Burrows is a zone of sand dunes which has grown up across the head of the bay. (Which direction did the wind come from?) In the protected area behind the dunes a zone of freshwater-marsh has developed, and the stream which flows through the marshes finds its way into the bay around the northern end of the dunes. The map symbols also show a wide area of foreshore at low tide (how wide?), and a wave-cut platform around Oxwich Point where erosion is very active. Copy the coastline of this area as

These dunes are part of Whitford Burrows, a nature conservation area on the north-west coast of the Gower Peninsula in South Wales. Marram grass has begun to stabilize and "fix" some of the dunes. Why do you think that visitors are not allowed to wander freely in such areas?

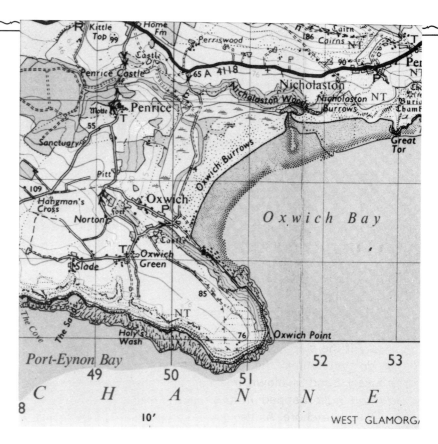

Oxwich Bay is on the south coast of the Gower Peninsula, an area of limestone cliffs and sandy bay-head beaches. This map extract is from O.S. Sheet 159 (1:50,000).

carefully as you can to make a map of your own, then add the following detail, using colour or symbols: offshore, intertidal zone, sand dunes, marsh, stream, wave-cut platform. Draw a key to explain your symbols and add a title "The Coast at Oxwich Bay".

Unlike salt-marshes, which are usually avoided by holiday crowds, sand dunes are very popular with visitors to the coast, and at the height of the season some dune areas become very congested. Can you think of any reasons why sand dunes should be so popular? Until about thirty years ago any areas of sand dunes which were a long way away from seaside resorts hardly had any visitors at all, but since then even the remotest areas of dunes attract their share of visitors. Why do you think this change has occurred?

When sand dune areas are intensively used by visitors erosion can occur. This usually begins near a path through the dunes, where the movement of lots of people is concentrated into one place. Constant trampling by thousands of feet can destroy the dune vegetation and when that happens there is nothing to bind the sand together. The on-shore winds which blew the grains of sand up from the shore in the first place can now pick them up again and blow them further inland. In this way a gully is formed across the dunes, called a "blow-out". If seaside visitors keep on using the path in large numbers, a huge gap will eventually be made, with a large area of wind-blown sand on the landward side.

When you visit an area of dunes, try to estimate how high they are and how large an area they cover. Which wind direction has been responsible for their formation? Is there an area of marsh behind them? How heavily are the dunes used for recreation? Is there evidence of erosion by "blow-outs"?

Geology at the Coast

The coast is often an exciting place for a geologist because the erosion carried out by waves provides so many opportunities for studying the rocks. If you live inland, the rocks in your area will probably be covered with soil and vegetation so, unless you can visit a quarry, say, you are unlikely to find places where you can study nicely exposed rock surfaces. At the coast, though, the cliffs and wave-cut platforms, and even the pebbles on the beaches, provide lots of opportunities for finding out about the rock materials of which they are made.

When you begin making your geological study it is helpful to think of the information you want in two parts. Firstly, you want to find out what *kind* of rocks make up your stretch of coast. In Britain we are lucky in having a great variety of rocks and this is one reason why we have such a variety of coastal scenery, for example, the white chalk cliffs of Kent and Sussex, the red sandstone cliffs of East Scotland and the dark igneous rocks of Land's End. Below is a list of the common rocks you might find around the coasts. Look these up in an encyclopaedia and write a paragraph about each of them.

The second set of geological information concerns the *structure* of the rocks, that is, the way rocks have been arranged, and possibly bent and broken, during the millions of years they have existed. As you saw on pages 14-15, the weakest parts of the rocks are eroded most quickly by the waves. When this happens the

Major Rock Types	Common Rock	Regional Examples
Sedimentary	Limestone	*Carboniferous Limestone*: Gower Peninsula, South Wales
		Magnesian Limestone: Durham coast
		Purbeck Limestone: Dorset
		Chalk: Flamborough Head, Yorkshire; Beachy Head, Sussex
	Sandstone	*Old Red Sandstone*: east coast of Scotland
		Wealden Sandstones: Hastings, Sussex
	Clays and Shales	*Kimmeridge Clay*: Isle of Purbeck
		Keuper Marl: north Somerset
		Weald Clay: Swanage Bay, Dorset
Igneous	Basalt	Giant's Causeway, Antrim, N. Ireland
	Granite	Land's End, Cornwall
	Volcanic	Isle of Skye, Scotland
Metamorphic	Schist	Start Point, south coast, Devon; north-west coast of Scotland

structure of the rocks is revealed for us to see.

Rocks are often formed in layers, called "strata", and some of these are harder than others. When the rock has been attacked by erosion the harder parts stand out and the softer parts are worn away. This process is called "differential erosion" and it is the cause of many of the irregularities you will find on the faces of cliffs.

Find out from a reference atlas or geology map in your library what kind of rocks are present at your part of the coast and find a place where you can study them. (If your coast is low-lying, with no rocks or cliffs, you will not be able to do this.) Look for rocks which have been washed clean and examine them closely, preferably with a hand magnifying-glass. Note any variation in detail (including colour) that you see. Look for examples of differential erosion and make sketches to illustrate the features which have been formed. If you are fortunate, you may find some fossils which you can draw and identify later from a reference book.

If your coast has a pebble beach, make a collection of as many different kinds of pebbles as you can and find out if they are made of the same kind of rock as the surrounding area. If they are different from the local rocks, how do you think they might have arrived on your beach? (Pages 8-9 will provide one explanation, but there could be others.)

These limestone cliffs on the south coast of Dorset have horizontal bedding planes and the effects of differential erosion are clear to see. Generally, the thicker strata stand out and appear more resistant to erosion.

In contrast to the horizontally bedded limestones, these sandstones on the foreshore of the Cornish coast near Bude show the effects of folding. The rocks have been crumpled by pressure forces within the earth's crust to form a small upfold or anticline. What evidence is there of differential erosion?

Boats

Boats are just as much a part of our image of the coast as the sea and the beaches. Although most of us may think of boats from the point of view of recreation, to many people they are a source of income. Apart from those who earn their living actually working on boats (such as fishermen), there are many others who depend on them too – people who build and repair boats, for example, or who supply equipment and fuel.

Boats have been used from the very earliest times as a form of transportation. In the days before we had modern roads and railways the easiest and cheapest way of taking goods from one end of Britain to the other was by sailing boat around the coast. The same wind energy which gives power to the waves also provides a free driving force for sailing boats. Nowadays commercial boats are usually driven by diesel engines and sailing boats are used mainly for recreation. The arrangement of masts and sails is known as the "rig" or "rigging" of a boat and many combinations have been tried on different kinds of boats. Find out from your library the names which are given to different sails, and make drawings of the various kinds of rigging.

Until fairly recently most boats were made from wood, but many are now made from fibre-glass, which is tough, light and cheap.

There are several different types of boat in the old harbour at Folkestone. Behind the shelter of the harbour breakwater there are fishing boats and some smaller pleasure craft. What are the probable destinations for the cross-Channel ferry tied up at the quayside?

Not all coastal settlements have sheltered harbours and here at Walmer on the east coast of Kent these small fishing boats are drawn up out of the sea for safety. In front of the boat on the left you can see one of the old winches used to pull the boats up the steep shingle beach.

Boat-building is a skilled craft, and people's lives depend on the ability of the boat-builder to make a boat strong enough to withstand buffeting by wind and waves and remain watertight. Find some boats which have been lifted from the sea and study the way the hull has been constructed. Make sketches of the way the sides of the boat have been joined together at the prow and at the stern.

Make a survey of the boats at your part of the coast and find out what they are used for. Make a list of all the different activities and occupations which are in any way connected with these boats. Large boats generally remain in the water all the time, but small boats are often removed from the sea when they are not being used – you may see whole rows of boats "beached" as in the photograph. Find out what method is used for getting them in and out of the water.

One of the nice things about boats is the way we give them names. Some names are serious, and some are meant to be amusing. Make a collection of names of boats and see if you can make any groups of different kinds. In addition to a name, some have a registration number. These help to identify the boat, and they can be used (like the registration number of a car) to find out more information about it. Fishing boats also have two letters in front of the registration number. These tell you the name of the home port – for example, RX means Rye, in Sussex. Make a note of any fishing boat registrations you see, and look them up in *Brown's Registrations* in the library. You can find out about larger boats too, by looking up the name in *Lloyd's Register of Shipping*. Any yachts with registration numbers can be traced in *Lloyd's Register of Yachts*.

Harbours

A harbour is a place where ships and boats can find shelter and protection from storms. Some harbours are "natural harbours" – in the estuary of a river, for example, or in the sheltered water behind a headland jutting out to sea. Where the coastline is too straight to give any natural protection, harbours can be made by building breakwaters out into the sea to make a sheltered area. These are called "artificial harbours".

The modern port of Hartlepool, in Cleveland, grew from a small fishing village which had its origin in a natural harbour. From the map you can see how the main protection is provided by a rocky headland called "The Heugh", and the original harbour was in a small creek called "The Slake". During the nineteenth century Hartlepool harbour grew in importance,

mainly because of coal exports from the Durham coalfield, and in 1847 a new West Harbour was built. Unlike the Old Harbour, the West Harbour is an artificial harbour and shelter is provided by the North Pier and South Pier. A breakwater on the headland gives protection from the severe gales which sometimes blow from the north-east, the direction of the greatest fetch.

Study a map of your harbour and work out where the most dangerous storms are likely to come from. You will have to consult an atlas to find out about the greatest fetch. What kind of natural protection is provided by the coastline? What additional shelter has been built? Draw a map to illustrate these details and add an arrow to show the direction of greatest fetch.

The responsibility for looking after a harbour belongs to the harbour authority. Sometimes this is a very large organization, like the Port of London Authority, for example, or the Tees and Hartlepool Port Authority. In the case of small harbours, the authority might be the local council, or a private company. The harbour authority appoints a Harbour Master

This is the small port of Watchet on the north coast of Somerset. The small harbour has been given extra protection by building a stone breakwater. What is the purpose of the timber and tyres on the harbour walls and quayside?

to look after the day-to-day running of the operations. The Harbour Master has to keep a daily log, including information about ships entering and leaving the harbour and the cargo they carry.

Find out which authority is responsible for your harbour and see if you can arrange a visit to talk to the Harbour Master. Each harbour publishes information for ships, for example, about the depth of water in the harbour and the size of ships that can be accommodated, tidal currents, the best way to approach the harbour, harbour signals, length of quays, the port services available and the harbour charges. Find this information and make a summary of it to put with your map. The old harbour log-books will be kept in the authority's archives. See if you can consult a log from, say, fifty years ago, and write an account of the changes which have taken place since then. Find out when the various parts of the harbour were constructed.

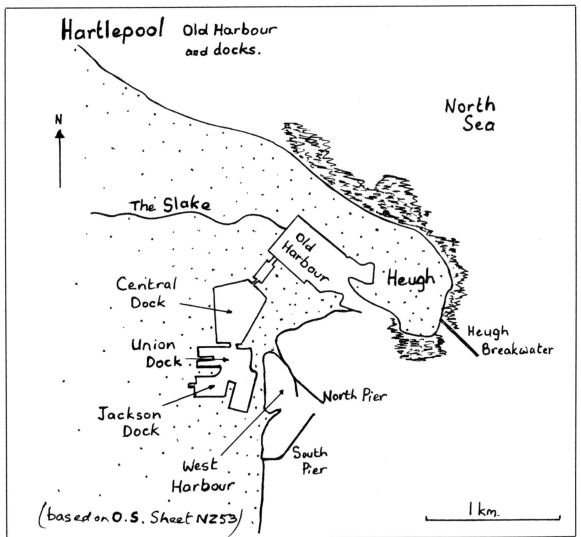

Hartlepool Old Harbour and docks.

N

North Sea

The Slake

Old Harbour

Heugh

Central Dock

Union Dock

Jackson Dock

Heugh Breakwater

North Pier

South Pier

West Harbour

(based on O.S. Sheet NZ53)

1 km.

The Holiday Season at the Coast

It is easy to understand why so many people enjoy a holiday at the seaside. The main attraction is the sea itself, of course, but the setting is important too and this varies with the character of the coast. You can pick your spot according to what kind of coast you like best. Think back to all the coastal features you have read about so far and then write a description of the kind of combination which would make your own ideal seaside.

Seaside holidays began to be fashionable when people thought that sea-bathing was good for the health, and they became very popular during the nineteenth century, following the growth of railways. Towns and cities in Victorian times were often grim places in which to live and a week at the seaside, or even a day-trip, provided a welcome break. Traditional links were made between certain resorts and industrial towns inland – Blackpool and the Lancashire industrial area, Cleethorpes and South Yorkshire, Southend and the East End of London, and many others.

Most seaside resorts developed along very similar lines. The beach was the main attraction with its seaside games, deck chairs and donkey rides. Overlooking the beach there

The holiday beach at Broadstairs, Kent, has been popular for a hundred years or more. Make a list of all the different types of things people have brought with them on to the beach. What facilities have been provided for the visitors?

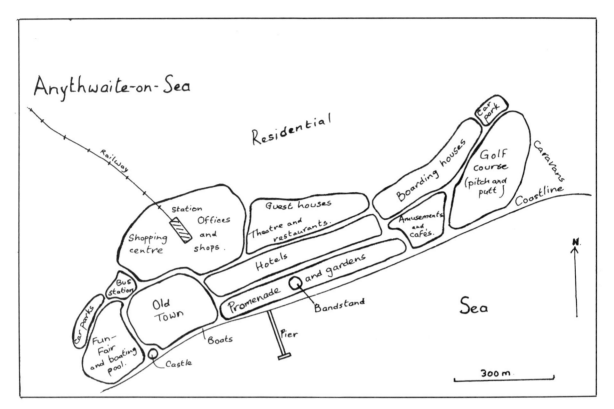

Anythwaite-on-Sea

Residential

Railway

Station
Offices
and
shops.

Shopping
centre

Guest houses

Theatre and
restaurants.

Boarding houses

Car park

Golf
course
(pitch and
putt)

Caravans

Coastline

Amusements
and
cafés.

Hotels

Bus
station

Old
Town

Promenade and gardens

Bandstand

Sea

N.

Car parks

Fun-
Fair
and boating
pool.

Boats

Pier

Castle

300 m.

would be a promenade with ornamental gardens, and coloured lights in the evening. There was often a pier and amusement arcades, theatre or fun-fair. Next there would be a row of hotels and boarding houses, with cafés and souvenir shops in the side-streets.

As the twentieth century has progressed, holiday habits have changed and seaside resorts have changed to suit them. Compared with a hundred years ago, or even fifty years ago, people nowadays have more money and more leisure time. Many people have cars. Fewer people stay in hotels and boarding houses; more stay in holiday camps and caravan sites. Because of this we use much more of the coast for holidays and recreation than we used to. There isn't the same concentration into seaside resorts that there was in the past when you could only get to the coast by train. On the other hand, many people go abroad and never visit the British seaside at all. Find out from your parents and grandparents, or any older people you know, which seaside places they used to visit and how they used to spend their time there. Make a list of your own activities at the seaside and write an account entitled "Seaside Holidays – Then and Now".

In many resorts, you will find a mixture of the old and the new. A typical example is shown in the map of Anythwaite-on-Sea. The layout of this imaginary resort is another "model", like the coastal features on pages 6-7. Make a survey of your resort and see how many of the features shown on the map you can find. Take a street map with you, mark on it the locations of the different areas and use this to draw your own map to compare with the model.

Recreation at the Coast

One of the great advantages of a holiday at the coast is the opportunity it provides for all kinds of recreation. For many people the main requirements are a deck-chair on the beach and a sunny day. Small children want to paddle and make sand castles. Almost everybody likes to lie in the sun. However, some people look for a more demanding, and perhaps more active recreation and the list on this page indicates the wide range of possibilities open to them.

Many forms of recreation are linked to the natural condition of the coast. Look back at all the various types of coast described in the earlier sections and consider which would be ideal for each of the activities on the list. Sometimes the ideal conditions will be a combination of two or more.

This is part of a small harbour used for mooring pleasure craft and fishing boats. Visitors can tow their boats to the coast by car and use the ramp to get the boats in and out of the water. Why is it important for visitors to know the state of the tide?

Some leisure pursuits require only a suitable setting in order for us to enjoy them — a level beach, say, or good waves. Other activities are greatly improved if special facilities are available — like a marina for sailing boats. Some need special equipment — an aqualung, for example, or a set of golf clubs. For some activities you need training and expert supervision. Check through the list again and

SWIMMING	BEACH GAMES
SCUBA DIVING	LAND SAILING
SURF-BOARDING	WATER SKI-ING
WIND SURFING	HORSE RIDING
SAILING	POWER-BOAT RACING
CLIMBING	BIRD WATCHING
FISHING	PAINTING, SKETCHING and PHOTOGRAPHY
GOLFING	RAMBLING
FOSSIL HUNTING	HANG GLIDING
TREASURE HUNTING	KITE FLYING

decide which of these various groups the activities fall into.

Other kinds of recreation and pastimes have nothing whatever to do with the physical nature of the coast, for instance, slot-machine games, bingo, fun-fairs, cinemas and theatrical entertainments. These usually come under the heading of "amusements". Where would you expect to find amusements like this in a seaside resort?

Take a notebook and pencil and make a detailed survey of all the recreational activities and amusements you can find. Make a note of any which make use of particular coastal zones (see pages 6-7). In those cases where there appears to be no link with the physical nature of the coast, try to work out what other reasons there might be for the choice of that particular location.

For some kinds of recreation the use of the coastal environment is free, but for others you have to pay. Surf-boarding is free (once you have bought your surf-board), but a round of

Why are fun-fairs and amusement arcades typical features of the seaside resort?

golf can be quite expensive. When you have to pay, the fee usually goes towards the cost of providing the facilities – in the case of golf, it helps to pay for the upkeep of the golf course. Which of the recreational activities on your list are free, and which ones do you have to pay for? Where you have to pay, what is the payment for?

In Britain the use of the seaside beaches is traditionally free. In many continental countries there are commercial sections of the beaches where you have to pay for access as well as amenities like beach-chairs and parasols or refreshments. Some parts of the beach may be taken over exclusively by beach "clubs" for children. Would you like to see this system used more in Britain? Discuss the advantages and disadvantages with your friends.

Overseas Links

When you are in a port you sometimes see notices in a foreign language. Beside the roads around Dover, for example, you will see "Tenez la gauche" and "Links fahren", which are the French and German ways of saying "Keep left", warning foreign visitors that the system in Britain is different from that on the continent. This is one indication that the coast is a place of contact with countries across the sea. In the United Kingdom the only international boundary on land is that between Northern Ireland and the Irish Republic. It is in the ports along the coast, therefore, that our links with foreign countries have to be organized and controlled (except, of course, links by air).

One of the overseas links is the movement of people in and out of the country. Some of these are holiday-makers – British people going abroad and foreigners coming in. Others are people travelling in the course of their job –

You must be able to follow signposts when you approach a port area! What is the role of the immigration office? What sort of documents are needed?

salesmen or lorry drivers, perhaps. Whoever they may be, it is important that the "immigration" authorities know when they have come in and gone out. Can you think of any reasons why?

Another important overseas link is trade – imports and exports. Every year the value of the food, materials and equipment that pass through our ports is billions of pounds. Much trade now goes by air, but most is still moved by sea, especially bulky and heavy things. Why do you think this is so? At the ports you will find equipment for loading and unloading ships, sheds for storage and railway sidings or roads for movement to and from the rest of the country.

It is the job of the customs officers to make sure that no goods are moved illegally in or out of the country and that the correct duties are paid. Most people meet with customs officials when they return from a holiday abroad, when they may have to open their luggage for inspection against smuggling. In the case of a ship, the customs officers go on board to inspect the cargo. Why do you think it is necessary to have customs checks? Find out from the Board of Customs and Excise what the regulations are for ordinary travellers.

The fact that Britain is an island has helped to keep us free from certain plant and animal diseases, so there are special regulations concerning the movement of animals and plants into the country. One of the most serious of these diseases is rabies. Find out about the problem of rabies from your local Department of Environmental Health and about the measures which are taken to prevent it reaching Britain.

Go to visit the nearest port on your part of the coast and look out for evidence of overseas links. Find out from the port authority what shipping contacts there are with foreign ports.

These are the docks at Swansea on the south coast of Wales and you can see the equipment and facilities needed at a dockside. Make a sketch of the photograph and label your picture with the following: breakwater; railway sidings; cranes; roads; warehouses; container lorries; swing bridge; dock-entrance; merchant ships; tug-boats; terraced housing.

Go to a travel agent and ask for copies of timetables for the ferry services between Britain and neighbouring continental countries (he won't mind giving you the ones that are just out of date). Find the ferry ports in your atlas, trace a map of the coastlines of Britain and the neighbouring countries, and mark in the ports. Join up all those which have connecting sailings.

Why are port authorities so worried about rabies?

Safety at the Coast

The coast can sometimes be a dangerous place and every year there are stories of accidents, some of which end in tragedy. Accidents will always happen, of course, but you can reduce the chances of having an accident if you understand what hazards you are facing and try your best to avoid them.

If you go round the bottom of a line of cliffs to explore a rock platform, you have to be careful to allow time to get back before high tide, in case your route back gets cut off by the rising water. Watching storm waves crashing onto the coast can be very exciting, but you have to be careful not to get too close or an extra-large wave might swamp you and the powerful undertow could drag you into the sea. Even in calm conditions people have been known to be swept out to sea on a lilo by an off-shore breeze or a strong current, and it doesn't need bad weather for weak swimmers to get out of their depth, or climbers to fall from cliffs. You can find out from the local police what particular hazards there are at your part of the coast.

The safety of ships and boats around the coast is the responsibility of several official bodies and organizations. Search and rescue operations for ships in distress are carried out by the men of the Coastguard Service, who keep constant watch around the coast and listen for calls of help on their radio. There are about 600 regular coastguards and about 9,000 voluntary, part-time coastguards. This service is run by the government and you can find out more about how it works and where the coastguard stations are by writing for information to the Department of Trade. You may also find this information in your library.

When the coastguards have located a ship in distress they can call for help from the lifeboats of the Royal National Lifeboat Institution (RNLI) and from the planes and helicopters of the armed forces. The RNLI is supported

This is the lighthouse on the shingle headland of Dungeness, Kent. What are the reasons for the lighthouse being so tall and painted in that way?

entirely by charity – perhaps you have bought a lifeboat sticker on an RNLI "flag-day". The map on the right shows the life-boat stations around the coasts of the British Isles. Each lifeboat has a crew of volunteers and there is always a local secretary. Find out from the secretary (you can get the name from the library) how the work of the lifeboat is organized, what kind of people serve as its crew, how it is called out and what rescue missions they have undertaken.

Another important safety organization is Trinity House, which looks after several hundred lighthouses, lightships and floating buoys around the coast. The lights are used to warn ships of special hazards like rocks and sand banks. If there is a lighthouse in your area, look out for it at night, and work out the timing of its sequence of flashes. Look up Trinity House in an encyclopaedia and write an account of how it started and what it does.

Lifeboat stations in 1980.

Aith
Lerwick

Stromness Kirkwall
Longhope
Thurso
Wick

Stornoway
Lochinver

Buckie Macduff
Invergordon Fraserburgh
Peterhead

Aberdeen
Stonehaven
Montrose

Barra Island

Mallaig Arbroath
Broughty Ferry

Oban Anstruther
North Berwick
Kinghorn St Abbs
Tighnabruaich Helensburgh Dunbar Berwick-upon-Tweed
Queensferry Eymouth
Islay North Sunderland
Craster
Largs Amble
Troon Newbiggin
Campbeltown Arran Blyth
Cullercoats Tynemouth
Girvan Sunderland
Portrush Red Bay Kirkcudbright Hartlepool Crimdon Dene
Arranmore Kippford Teesmouth Redcar
Portpatrick Stranraer Silloth Staithes and Runswick Whitby
Bangor Workington Scarborough
Donaghadee St Bees Filey
Cloughey-Portavogie Flamborough
Portaferry Ramsey Bridlington
Newcastle Peel Barrow Morecambe
Port Erin Douglas Withernsea
Clogher Head Port St Mary Fleetwood Humber
Blackpool
Lytham St Anne's
Howth Mablethorpe
Dun Laoghaire Hoylake Skegness
Llandudno Rhyl Hunstanton
Moelfre New Brighton Wells Sheringham
Holyhead West Kirby Cromer
Trearddur Bay Conwy Happisburgh
Wicklow Beaumaris Flint Great Yarmouth
Porthdinllaen Criccieth and Gorleston
Arklow Pwllheli Lowestoft
Abersoch Barmouth Southwold
Aberdovey
Dunmore East Kilmore Borth Aldeburgh
Tramore Rosslare Aberystwyth
Youghal Harbour New Quay Harwich
Fishguard Cardigan Walton and Frinton
way Bay St David's Tenby West Mersea Clacton-on-Sea
Valentia Little and Broad Haven Burnham-on-Crouch
Ballycotton Angle The Mumbles Southend-on-Sea Margate
Courtmacsherry Burry Port Port Talbot Ramsgate
altimore Harbour Porthcawl Sheerness Walmer
Horton and Port Eynon St Donats Whitstable Dover
Minehead Penarth Littlestone-on-Sea
Barry Dock Dungeness
Clovelly Ilfracombe Weston-super-Mare Hayling Island Rye Harbour
Appledore Portsmouth Brighton Hastings
Lymington Eastbourne
Bude Calshot Newhaven
Padstow Port Isaac Mudeford Shoreham Harbour
Newquay Poole Littlehampton
St Agnes Lyme Regis Weymouth Yarmouth Selsey
St Ives Exmouth Swanage Bembridge
Fowey Torbay
Sennen Cove Salcombe
Falmouth Plymouth
Penlee Lizard—Cadgwith
St Mary's

St Peter Port
St Catherine's St Helier

If you have ever been on a sea voyage, even a short one across the English Channel, you may have wondered how the ship's captain can find his way into port so precisely. Modern technology, of course, is of enormous help – the ship's radar will give accurate details of the position of the coast and of any other vessels nearby, echo sounders will show the depth of the water, and radio signals can be used to indicate direction. Once a ship approaches the land, however, the captain needs to know the detailed layout of the coast and the sea-bed so that he can plot a safe course past any hazards. He also has to know about the variations in the tide and any tidal currents which may sweep him off-course. For this information he has to consult a "chart" of the coast. For any small ships or boats without the technical gadgets, charts are the only navigational aids.

A chart is like a map but, unlike on a map, many of the details shown are things you cannot see, because they are under the water. The information on a chart has been gradually built up over many years – hundreds of years, perhaps – from the observations made by generations of mariners and from special surveys. The charts of the coasts of Britain are very detailed and very accurate. The best charts are the Admiralty Charts, which contain the greatest detail. Other charts are based on the Admiralty Charts.

The basic information on a chart is the depth of water and the shape of the coast, though there is much more in addition. Off the coast of Norfolk, for example, the charts show the position of the pipelines bringing North Sea gas to the shore. All charts show lighthouses, lightships and navigational buoys. Prominent features on the land which can be used for navigation are also marked, like water towers and church spires. The tidal range at each part of the coast is provided in special tables,

together with the speed of the tidal currents. If there are special instructions for approaching a particular harbour, these too will be given.

The chart of the coast around Scarborough is part of a yachting chart for the east coast of England. Study the chart and the key below, then answer the following questions: How wide is the entrance to the Old Harbour? What is the shallowest depth of water you would find on your way into harbour? What hazards are there along the coast to the north and south of Scarborough? What would you know if you saw a Black ball shown from the Vincent Pier Lighthouse? When should you *not* attempt to enter the harbour?

Now find out what the charts can tell you about navigation along your stretch of coast. (Charts are fairly expensive to buy, but you can consult them in a library).

	KEY
◸◹◺◿	cliffed coastline
〰	rocky foreshore
✳	rock which is uncovered at LW
+	underwater rock
Chy	chimney
LB	lifeboat
Lt Ho	lighthouse
Tr	tower

Navigation chart for Scarborough, published by Imray Laurie Norie and Wilson Ltd. The figures show soundings in metres at lowest astronomical tide.

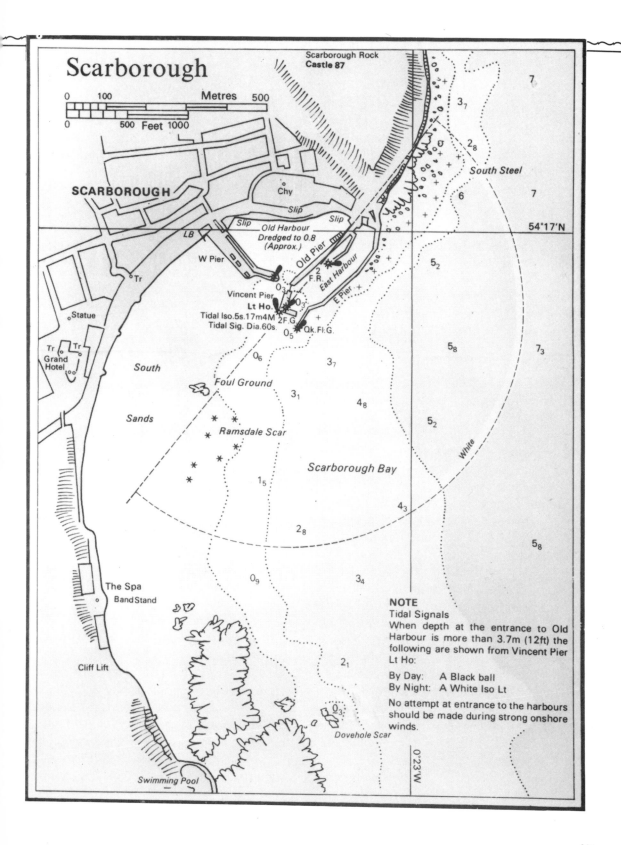

Scarborough

Metres 0 100 500

Feet 0 500 1000

Scarborough Rock
Castle 87

SCARBOROUGH

Chy

Slip

Slip   Slip

Old Harbour
Dredged to 0.8
(Approx.)

Old Pier

LB

W Pier

0_3

2
F.R.

East Harbour

E Pier

Vincent Pier

Lt Ho.
Tidal Iso.5s.17m4M
Tidal Sig. Dia.60s.

0_3

2 F.G.

0_5 Qk.Fl.G.

Tr

0_6

3_7

0_5

0_6

South

Foul Ground

3_1

4_8

Statue

Tr   Tr
Grand Hotel

Sands

✱ ✱
Ramsdale Scar
✱ ✱
✱ ✱
✱

1_5

Scarborough Bay

2_8

The Spa
Band Stand

0_9

3_4

Cliff Lift

2_1

0_3
Dovehole Scar

Swimming Pool

Scarborough Rock
Castle 87

7

3_7

2_8

South Steel

7

6

54°17'N

5_2

5_8

7_3

5_2

White

4_3

5_8

NOTE
Tidal Signals
When depth at the entrance to Old
Harbour is more than 3.7m (12ft) the
following are shown from Vincent Pier
Lt Ho:

By Day: A Black ball
By Night: A White Iso Lt

No attempt at entrance to the harbours
should be made during strong onshore
winds.

0°23'W

Reclamation

Compared with many countries, Britain is quite small – about 244,000 square kilometres. With about 55 million inhabitants this means an average of more than 200 persons for every square kilometre. When you travel around you may get the impression that there is plenty of spare land – for new houses, for example, or factories, or roads. But the more we build, the less land there is for other things, especially agriculture. Land in Britain is scarce, so we have to make the best use of what we have. Sometimes we have opportunities to increase our land area by reclaiming land from the sea.

As you saw on pages 18-19, some parts of the coast are gradually being built up out of the sea by deposition. Every bit of salt-marsh that grows means an extra bit of land added to the coast. Unfortunately, this natural process takes such a long time that it is of no practical use. However, if we can help to speed up this natural process, the reclamation of land from the sea becomes a real possibility.

People have been reclaiming land from the sea around Britain since the Middle Ages. In principle, the method is simple. You find an area of salt-marsh or tidal mud-flats and build a wall around it to keep the sea out. The difficulty lies in building the sea-wall (or "dyke") big and strong enough to keep the sea out permanently, even during storms. To do this successfully requires great engineering skill and it costs a great deal of money. It is not surprising that reclamation in early times was carried out just one or two fields at a time.

When land is protected by a sea-wall, some method has to be found of allowing the water in the rivers to drain away into the sea. This is done by building "sluice-gates" in the sea-wall. A sluice-gate is like a small dam which can be raised and lowered. If there are any low-lying areas of land at your part of the coast, see if you can find any sluice-gates where the

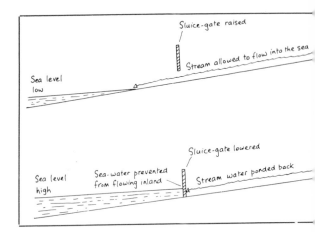

How a sluice-gate works.

streams flow into the sea. These might be evidence to show that the land has been reclaimed.

The most spectacular examples of coastal reclamation are in Holland. The Dutch are the experts and we use the Dutch word "polder" to describe an area of land reclaimed from the sea. They have been so successful that they have increased their land area by nearly a half. Find out more about the Dutch polders from the reference books in your library.

We have nothing in Britain to compare with the size of the reclaimed areas in Holland. The largest area of reclaimed land in Britain is the Fens, just inland from the Wash, along the east coast. Most of the Fens were reclaimed as long ago as the seventeenth and eighteenth centuries. Numerous other examples can be found, usually around the mouths of estuaries where sheltered conditions have allowed sand and mud to accumulate. The most important area of modern reclamation is Seal Sands at the mouth of the River Tees in Cleveland. Find out more about the Fens and Seal Sands from your library. Can you think of any groups of people, or organizations, who may be against reclaiming mud-flats and salt-marshes?

This view is taken from Brean Down, a distinctive headland south of Weston-super-Mare, Avon. The photograph shows the estuary of the River Axe and the farmland extends out on to the coastal flats. On the right-hand side of the winding sea-wall the land has been reclaimed, but to the left the original salt-marsh remains and is still covered by the sea at periods of very high tide.

This used to be an area of tidal mud-flats and a haven for migrating wildfowl. The area has been reclaimed by building up the level of the land with industrial waste. The surface has been raised by about 3 metres. What type of industry can you see in the distance?.

Coastal Protection

People who live and work at the coast have to take precautions against the damage which can be caused by the sea. We have already seen some of the things that can be done to reduce the effect of the processes at work – the building of groynes, for example, to prevent a beach being washed away, or a breakwater to improve the shelter of a harbour. Every now and then, though, an exceptional storm catches the news headlines with a story of destruction and, possibly, loss of life.

The photograph on the right shows what happened during a storm in 1978 at the holiday village of Torcross in Devon. On that occasion mountainous waves crashed right across the beach into the buildings along the sea-front

and thousands of pounds-worth of damage was caused. Such a storm may not strike again for fifty years, but there is also a chance that it might happen again next year.

The most serious threat is to the east coast of England and it comes from what is known as a "tidal surge" in the North Sea. A tidal surge is produced by a combination of northerly gales and high spring tides. The gales from the north cause the water to pile up towards the south. This piling-up is increased by the narrowing of the North Sea at its southern end. Surges of 1.8 metres are possible, and when this coincides with a spring tide the result along low-lying coasts can be catastrophic. In 1952 huge areas of the east coast were flooded by a tidal surge and the cost of the damage was put at millions of pounds.

After 1952 it was realized that a similar tidal surge could cause a major disaster in London. Not only would the damage be enormous (e.g. to buildings and the London Underground), but many thousands of people might be drowned. This threat has been removed by the building of the Thames Barrier near Woolwich. The barrier can be raised from the river bed to prevent the surge from reaching London. A similar threat to the low-lying centre of Hull, in Humberside, led to the building of a barrier there too, shown in the photograph.

Find out what steps have been taken at your part of the coast to protect land and property from damage and floods. Study an Ordnance Survey map (1:50,000) to locate areas that are low-lying and find out if there is a sea-wall to hold back extra-high tides. Find out from the council if any engineering works have been carried out to protect any parts of the coast from erosion. Go and see what has been done and what materials have been used. Write to the Greater London Council (GLC) to find out more about the Thames Barrier.

"Tidal surge". When and where atmospheric pressure is low, the sea-level is higher and with gales blowing from the north this "mound" of sea is pushed south. Because the southern end of the North Sea is narrower and shallower, this tidal surge can cause the sea-level to rise dramatically along the coasts and estuaries.

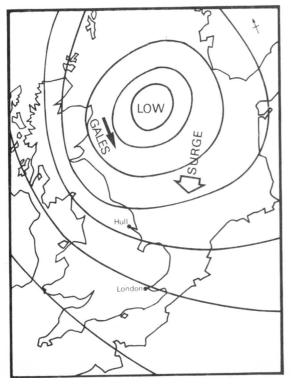

Torcross is a small row of houses built on a shingle ridge. There is no defence from heavy seas. What do you think makes it impossible to build a sea-wall along this piece of coastline?

The tidal surge barrier on the River Hull was opened in April 1980. When there is a threat of tidal flooding the gate suspended above the river between the towers can be lowered to keep the flood waters out of the city and its industrial areas.

Coastal Pollution

In recent years people have gradually become more aware that the pollution of the environment is a serious problem. At the very least, pollution causes unpleasantness and spoils our enjoyment of the environment – like unsightly litter. At the worst, pollution caused by some wastes is so poisonous that it could remain dangerous for thousands of years – like nuclear waste. Unfortunately, there is no way that we can stop producing all waste. To do that we should have to close most of our factories and stop using fuels. Even then we should still have the problem of human waste (i.e. sewage). So we have to accept that some wastes cannot be avoided and try to make sure that they cause the least possible damage to the environment and to wildlife.

In the past, many companies deliberately built their factories near the coast so that they

Just look at the variety of plastic bottles and containers on this isolated stretch of beach in Worbarrow Bay on the south coast of Dorset. Why is plastic litter such a particular nuisance? How do you think we could solve this problem of litter?

could get rid of the waste liquids (called "effluent") by simply pouring them into the sea. At many places along the coast, especially in estuaries, the effluents from industries like steel works and chemicals factories produced so much pollution that fish and other natural life in the water died. Nowadays the government is gradually bringing in regulations to reduce this kind of pollution and life is beginning to recover in the estuaries.

One of the main causes of coastal pollution in Britain is oil from the thousands of tankers which carry it in from places like the Middle East. International regulations now prevent tankers from deliberately polluting the sea, but accidents sometimes happen which cause spillages. When that happens, oil or tar is swept onto the coast, beaches are ruined by the black, smelly mess, and sea birds die in their thousands. Even small patches of tar can be a nuisance on a holiday beach, sticking to feet and spoiling clothes.

Many coastal towns still get rid of their sewage by pumping it into the sea. It usually goes out quite a long way, through a pipe, but it can sometimes be unpleasant. In Britain we are fortunate in having two tides each day which help to sweep wastes away (though they sometimes sweep them back onto the beach too!) In the Mediterranean Sea, where there are scarcely any tides, the problem of coastal pollution is much greater.

Find out from the Environmental Health Department of the local council whether there are any sewage or industrial waste outlets along your part of the coast. Walk along the beach, along the strand-line left by the tide, and make a list of all the materials there. Which ones do you consider to be "pollution" and which ones do you not mind about? Make a survey of the amount of litter on the beach and promenade and find out whether there are any particularly bad spots. Can you find any explanation for these? Find out whether there are enough litter bins and whether they are in the best positions.

Pollution of the coast is not only by oil and liquid effluents. Along the North Sea coast of Durham coalmines have tipped their waste into the sea for nearly a hundred years. The small fragments of coal in the waste are separated out by the action of the waves and, after each high tide, people go to the beach to collect "sea coal" for use at home.

Heritage Coasts

When we talk of our "national heritage" we could mean a great many things – famous old buildings, perhaps, or the work of famous British artists and writers, or even our ancient traditions. Our heritage consists of all the things that are important to us, as a nation of people, that are handed down to us from the past, and which we want to keep and remember. Our scenery is part of that heritage too, especially scenery which seems to us to be particularly beautiful. Much of our finest scenery is the combination of land and sea which we find at the coast. Which kind of coastal scenery do you like best?

Unfortunately, because of the way more and more of the coast is being used up (for houses, factories, camp-sites, etc), we are in danger of losing much of our heritage of coastal scenery. As long ago as 1965 the National Trust began a project to buy stretches of beautiful coast and preserve them on behalf of the nation. This project was called "Enterprise Neptune". The National Trust now owns more than 600 kilometres of coast. However, the National Trust is a charity and it cannot possibly be expected to look after the entire coast.

The government itself has now stepped in to try to preserve the remaining stretches of unspoiled coast. Any local authority which has a beautiful stretch of coast within its boundaries can treat it as a "Heritage Coast". This means that the council would do its best to prevent any developments on the coast which might spoil its natural character. Find out from the Planning Department of your local authority whether they have any Heritage Coasts, and how they plan to look after them.

There are problems of conservation on all coasts, whether they are especially attractive or not. Some of these problems are caused by conflicts between groups of people who want different things. It is natural, for example, for people to want to have caravans near the coast, so that they can enjoy a seaside holiday. Other people believe that caravan parks spoil the scenery. The answer to this kind of problem is to "manage" the coast. Councils can do this by making a plan for each section after carrying out a thorough survey of all the various ways people want to use the coast.

See if you can make a management plan for

The heavily marked lines indicate the Heritage Coasts of Great Britain. There are in England and Wales alone more than 35 separate pieces of coastline protected by local authorities, a total distance of over 1200 km. Which parts of Great Britain have the smallest amounts of Heritage Coast? Why is this?

your stretch of coast. First you have to make a survey to find out what is there, so don't choose too much – a kilometre will be enough. Walk along the coast and make a note of all the ways the coast is used from the sea itself up to about 200 metres inland from the backshore. Do this with a group of your friends. Then you can discuss which kind of plan you think is best. You will probably argue about it, too.

This coastal area of south Dorset, just west of Lulworth Cove, is a Heritage Coast. Do you feel that the caravans are a threat to the beauty of this landscape and spoil the view?

Lulworth Cove is an outstanding stretch of coastal scenery attracting thousands of visitors. In the summer season the area of parked cars (centre) is three times as large, extending along the valley; people swarm over the beach, the hillsides and the coastal paths. How can we stop places like this being spoilt by overcrowding?

Difficult Words

backwash	The water which runs back down the beach after a wave breaks.
beach	The gently sloping accumulations of sand and shingle which are found along the coast where the sea meets the land. The beach extends from the low-tide mark to the highest point reached by storm waves.
bedding planes	The surfaces which separate distinctive layers of rock. Bedding planes appear as "lines" on a cliff face or exposure of rock and reveal the structure of the rocks, i.e. the way in which the rock layers have been folded or faulted.
berm	A narrow shelf or ridge of shingle thrown up on the beach by storm waves. Shingle beaches often have 2 or 3 distinct ridges or berms, each marking a different storm level. These remain until a later storm re-shapes the beach materials into a new berm.
blow-out	A hollow in an area of sandy material, especially amongst sand dunes or heathland, which is formed by the wind blowing the sand away. Blow-outs can be progressively enlarged by the wind to form deep depressions.
breakwater	A structure built to protect the coast by lessening the force of the waves as they break against the shore. Typical breakwaters are constructed of timber and are built at right-angles to the coastline in order to slow down the movement of beach materials along the coast (see long-shore drift).
conservation	The controlled use of things which are themselves growing or subject to change, like soil, forests, mineral deposits or wildlife habitats and human landscapes. Conservation requires thoughtful planning and controls to ensure the continued or extended use of a resource, such as coal or a place of historic or scenic value.
cusp	A crescent-shaped accumulation of shingle on the beach, with the points of the crescent pointing to the sea. There is, generally, very evident sorting of material, with sand and the finest shingle in the centre of the cusp and larger shingle forming the small crescentic ridge (see pages 12-13).
energy	The energy created by wind and waves is the power to do "work". The energy of the waves is used to erode the coastline, to transport beach materials and to break boulders and pebbles into smaller and smaller rounded pieces.
erosion	The wearing away and removal of rock by running water, ice, wind and waves. These are the agents of erosion.
fault	A break or fracture of the rock strata caused by movements in the Earth's crust. The location of a fault can often be picked out in a cliff face when a break or line of dislocation interrupts a regular pattern of bedding planes.
fetch	The distance of open water over which a wind-blown ocean wave has travelled, or over which a wind blows. The fetch helps to determine the height and energy of a wave; generally, the longer the fetch, the bigger and stronger the waves.
geologist	A person who studies the rocks and structures of the Earth's crust.
head	The head of a bay is its most landward point furthest from the two headlands which lie on either side of the bay.
high water	The point and time at which the incoming tide reaches its highest level. After the point of high water the sea level then gradually falls as the tide goes out.
igneous rocks	Rocks formed by the cooling and solidification of molten rock (magma). Volcanic rocks are igneous.
inter-tidal	The inter-tidal zone is the area of the shore between low tide and high tide. The inter-tidal range is the vertical height difference between the average levels of low and high tides.
joints	Small cracks or fractures in rock which are usually at right-angles to the bedding planes.
long-shore drift	The movement of beach materials along the coast, caused by waves approaching the shoreline at an oblique angle.
metamorphic rocks	Rocks which have been altered in their chemical composition and appearance by the great heat and pressure deep in the Earth's crust.
polder	A piece of low-lying land at or below sea-level which has been reclaimed from the sea.
pollution	The introduction by people of waste and other products in sufficient quantities to cause damage to the environment.

promenade	A paved area at the sea front along which people can walk or "promenade" to enjoy the sea air. Many promenades with formal gardens were built in the nineteenth century as the popularity of seaside holidays grew.
quarry	A large pit or hole in the ground made when digging out useful rocks such as granite for building-stone or chalk for making cement.
reef	A mass of rocks with their surface at or just above the level of low tide.
relief	The shape of the land with its hills and valleys. The variations in the height above sea-level of the land surface.
salt-marsh	A coastal marsh along a low-lying shore, often found in the sheltered part of a river estuary or behind an offshore sand-spit.
sand dunes	Accumulations of sand which are moved and shaped by the wind. Plants such as marram grass help to fix the dunes in one place by binding the sand together with their roots.
sedimentary rocks	Rocks consisting of sediments laid down in layers, generally on the floor of a lake or ocean, and later solidified to form rocks like sandstone.
stack	A steep-sided pillar of rock rising from the sea which earlier was part of the land until isolated by wave erosion.
strand-line	Another term for shore-line, the margin between land and sea.
strata	Layers of sedimentary rock.
structure	The way in which sedimentary rocks are arranged by the processes of folding and faulting. An anticline is a structure where rocks have been folded upwards by pressure forces within the Earth's crust.
swash	The mass of foaming water which rushes up the beach as a wave breaks.
tidal range	The average difference in vertical height between the water levels of high tide and low tide.
tidal surge	The strong flow of water caused by the incoming tide, especially when the flow is constricted by an estuary or narrowing of a channel. The effect of a tidal surge can be greatly increased by a following wind.

Book List

Books marked with an asterisk (*) are most suitable for the teacher's use only.

Angel, H., *Life on the Seashore,* Macmillan Educational, 1976

Automobile Association, *Illustrated Guide to the Coast,* Drive Publications, A.A., 1984

Bellamy, D. (Ed.), *Coastal Walks,* Hamlyn, 1982

Benson, B., *Ships,* Macdonald Educational, 1975

*Bentley, J.C. and Charlton, W.A., *The Use of Maps in School,* Basil Blackwell, 1975

*Brown, J.H., *Elementary Geographical Fieldwork,* Blackie, 1978

*Countryside Commission, *The Coastal Heritage,* HMSO, 1970

Dee Estuary Conservation Group, *The Dee Estuary,* D.E.C.G., 1976

Department of Trade, *United Kingdom Maritime Search and Rescue Organisation,* HMSO, 1979

Dunning, F.W. et. al., *Britain before Man,* Geological Museum, HMSO, 1978

*Galbraith, I., *Map Reading and Analysis,* OUP, 1979

Hamilton, W.R., *Minerals, Rocks and Fossils,* Country Life Books, Hamlyn, 1980

Howarth, P., *Lifeboat,* Hamlyn, 1981

Hutson, T., *Yearbook of Tall Ships,* Faber, 1978

Jackman, L., *The Beach,* Evans, 1974

Jackman, L., *Exploring the Seashore,* Evans, 1970

Kemp, P., *The Oxford Companion to Ships and the Sea,* OUP, 1976

*Knapp, B.J., *Earth and Man,* Allen and Unwin, 1982

*Mills, D., *Geographical Work in Primary and Middle Schools,* Geographical Association, 1981

Scarlett, B., *Shipminder,* Pelham Books Limited, 1971

Thackray, J., *British Fossils,* Geological Museum, HMSO, 1984

Webb, W., *Coastguard,* HMSO, 1976

Williams, B., *Ships and other Seacraft,* Kingfisher Books, 1983

Index